W9-BAS-829

ATLANTIC LIGHT

THE WEST COAST OF IRELAND IN PHOTOGRAPHS

Image opposite: Tory Island, Co. Donegal

ATLANTIC LIGHT

THE WEST COAST OF IRELAND IN PHOTOGRAPHS

For my mother, who gave me the push
I needed to send me in the right direction.

Ireland's West Coast

There is nothing that inspires me so much as the coast of Ireland, and the west coast in particular. I grew up by the sea, in Dún Laoghaire just south of Dublin. The east coast is beautiful and can certainly be wild when the mood takes it, but it can't hold a candle to the drama and scale of the west.

In 2014, Fáilte Ireland, the national tourism agency, created a new driving route along this coastline. Called the Wild Atlantic Way, it extends from Kinsale in the south to Malin Head in the north. A distance of about 430 kilometres as the crow flies, the coastal route is a whopping 2,500 kilometres. This route has served to open up large areas of coastline to tourism that previously had seen very little. The roads have always been there, but the new signage encourages exploration like never before.

As a landscape photographer, I never met a bóithrín (small road) that I didn't want to drive down, so many of these tracks I was aware of, and even regarded as little private finds—especially those in the southwest, where I live! It's a great thing that these little wonders are now more easily accessible by others.

I've often said to the people I take on photography workshops that every part of the west coast has a different character to every other. From the low rounded hills of Cork, we follow the peninsulas to the higher and more jagged mountains of Kerry. Next it's across the Shannon Estuary into Clare and its karst limestone landscape and the sheer Cliffs of Moher. Further north still, we have the low-lying coast of Connemara in Galway, punctuated by the Twelve Bens just inland.

Forming the border between Galway and Mayo is Killary Harbour, Ireland's only fjord, which is bordered on its north side by Mweelrea, the highest mountain in the province of Connaught. As we travel north, we come to Clew Bay and its islands, guarded by the imposing bulk of Clare Island at its mouth. The sacred mountain of Croagh Patrick dominates the landscape for miles around.

It's not too much further to Achill Island, Ireland's largest offshore island with its impressive mountains and massive sea cliffs. This is contrasted by low-lying Belmullet just to its north, almost an island in its own right, but connected to the mainland by a narrow isthmus.

To go north now, we must first travel east along the north coast of Mayo, passing the Céide Fields, an ancient neolithic field system, preserved under the bog that swallowed it thousands of years ago. Nearby is Downpatrick Head, where 25 members of the 1798 rising took refuge in a blowhole beneath the cliffs. They were drowned by the incoming tide before the ladder could be brought back to let them out.

Onward still is Benbulben, the most identifiable of Ireland's mountains, where the legendary Fionn Mac Cumhaill led Diarmuid to his death at the tusks of the Wild Boar. Here, we turn north towards Donegal, which rises wild and unforgiving to the holy mountain of Slieve League and its cliffs.

Close to the end of our journey, we pass towering headlands and Arranmore Island before arriving at Tory Island, the most northerly of the still-inhabited offshore islands. It was here that Balor of the Evil Eye locked his daughter Ethniu away at Dún Bhaloir to prevent her from bearing him a grandson, who it was prophesied would kill him. Naturally, that did no good and he was killed by Lugh, her son, in battle.

Our last stop is the island of Inishtrahull, the northernmost part of Ireland which, like the Fastnet rock in the south, is known as the Teardrop of Ireland. Emigrating families who left from the north of the country would pass this island and with it, their last sight of home. For many, they would never come back.

It's difficult not to be inspired by such a coastline. Between the highlights are countless beaches, bays, cliffs, and coves that are unknown and unremarked, but each one is beautiful and full of potential.

I hope you enjoy this book, which only scratches the surface of what can be seen on this wonderful coast. A full study would take many years, and I look forward to continuing my own.

Notes on Aerial Photography

Before I moved home to Ireland in 2005, I had spent ten years living in Chicago, in the US. While I was there, I earned my private pilot's license and flew both fixed-wing aeroplanes and small helicopters. I love to fly, and the views from the air always fascinated me. Unfortunately, as a pilot, the options for photography are limited—there are a few other things on your mind!

When I moved home, the cost of flying became prohibitive, and I had turned my passion towards photography full time. However, I was lucky to be able to incorporate my love of flying with this new career and I started to learn how to effectively compose images from this platform.

Towards the end of 2013, drone technology was on the rise. While most drones carried only small cameras that couldn't produce the sort of high technical quality I require in my photographs, I could see that it should be possible to build one that would carry a DSLR camera. I did some research and placed an order for a custom-built vehicle to do just that.

Unfortunately, the trouble with using bleeding-edge technology is that often things don't go as well as you'd like. Several months and many problems later, it became obvious that this wasn't going to work. I was forced to abandon this machine and look elsewhere.

Thankfully, the technology had continued to develop while I was struggling with my first drone, and a turnkey solution was on the market that could carry the exact camera I was using for my ground-based photography at the time, the Canon 5D Mk III. The lens choice was limited to just a fixed 24mm f/2.8 optic, but as this was my preferred focal length for aerial work, I was quite happy. I finished the paperwork needed for my license and aerial works permit from the Irish Aviation Authority and set to work.

I knew that I was going to use my aerial photography as a major part of my next book, and took the new drone for its maiden flight on the first of my dedicated trips for the book. I started in Donegal, my logic being that it was best to start at the most distant location and to work my way south.

I live in Cork, in the south of the country, so each trip should, in theory, be easier than the last one. Of course, this wasn't the case, and I ended up making the last images for the book in Donegal again!

The first photograph I made with the new aerial rig was Banba's Crown on page 121. It was the very first flight of the drone, and as with most of the images in the book, required taking the drone out over the Atlantic. No matter how many times I do this, it always makes me nervous. Drone technology is not particularly mature, and things do go wrong. From curious birds to sudden strong wind gusts to simple mechanical or electrical failure, there are many and more things that can go wrong. If a problem happens over water, there's not even any wreckage that can be recovered, and even if there was, everything of importance would be ruined by salt water.

I had my share of setbacks, but in the end was able to complete the book. Not all images here are made with a drone, although the majority are. I've been lucky enough to fly with the Commissioners of Irish Lights on several occasions and have photographed most of the offshore lighthouses from their helicopter. I've also chartered my own helicopter and fixed-wing flights for photographs both onshore and off.

Clearly, flying a drone has significant advantages. It's vastly cheaper than "real" aircraft time, as well as being far more flexible. I can take a chance on the weather with the drone, arriving at a location at sunrise with a dubious weather forecast—something I'd never risk with the money involved in a helicopter charter. But it's often in those sorts of conditions that the best images are made.

Full-size aircraft excel with range and altitude. Drones are limited by regulations in how high they can fly and how far away, and they have limited battery life at any rate. Fifteen minutes of flight is about as much as you can expect with today's technology.

The other advantage enjoyed by full-size aircraft right now is flying in all weathers. The drones of today have no weatherproofing, and all the electronics are exposed to the elements. Even a light shower can have disastrous consequences, perhaps not on the flight where it occurs, but corrosion can cause a failure days or weeks later.

Old Head of Kinsale, County Cork

The Old Head is one of the more prominent peninsulas on the coast and has been home to lighted beacons for over two thousand years. Kinsale is also the beginning of the Wild Atlantic Way, the coastal driving route that follows the west coast of Ireland all the way up to the northern tip of Donegal.

Lighthouses hold a special fascination for me. There's a real sense of heroism about them, these towers placed in seemingly impossible locations, perched above stormy seas.

It's off this headland that the Lusitania was torpedoed and sunk in 1915 with the loss of 1,200 passengers.

Phase One IQ180, Phase One 35mm f/3.5

f/5, 1/500 at ISO 200

Inchydoney, County Cork

Inchydoney is an island, now connected by a pair of causeways to the mainland. It's a popular tourist location and holiday destination, particularly among Irish people. It's well known for its wonderful beaches, one on each side of the headland.

This image is one of my favourites in this book. Like many such photographs, it was entirely unplanned. I was flying over the beach and decided to direct the camera straight down to capture the patterns of the waves lapping on the low-lying sand. I noticed a man walking his dog, and used him as the anchor for the composition.

Canon EOS 5D Mk III, EF24mm f/2.8 IS USM
f/4, 1/200 at ISO 100

Galley Head, County Cork

In 1849 and 1857 two attempts were made to build a light at Galley Head, both rebuffed for financial reasons by Trinity House, the organization in the UK that is responsible for lighthouses around the coast. Finally, in 1871, after the number of wrecks off the headland had further increased, Trinity House relented and agreed to the construction of a light. It was completed in 1878 and has been in operation ever since.

In 2002, the old Keepers' dwellings, which are no longer needed since the light was automated in 1979, were re-furbished and can now be rented by anyone who wants to live a few days on the cliffs over the sea. And who can argue with the views?

Canon EOS 5D Mk III, EF24mm f/2.8 IS USM

f/2.8, 1/500 at ISO 100

Rabbit Island, County Cork

Like many of the uninhabited small islands that dot the south coast of Cork, Rabbit Island was once inhabited. The remains of a house can be seen on the south shore, and the field boundaries are obvious.

No one has lived here in many a year, however. Nor does anyone care about gathering the seaweed around its shore, which was once a selling point of this tiny island in an 1850 advertisement.

This morning looked like there would be no sunrise to speak of, but persistence paid off with a small gap in the clouds in just the right spot. That was the only time the sun came out all day!

Canon EOS 5D MK III, EF24mm f/2.8 IS USM

f/2.8, 1/30 at ISO 200

The Fastnet Rock, County Cork

By far the most famous lighthouse on the Irish coast, the Fastnet is also the southernmost point of Ireland. It lies 6.5 kilometres to the southwest of Cape Clear Island, the southernmost inhabited island (visible at the top of the image).

Pictured is the second of two lighthouses that were built here. The black cylinder on the rock behind the tower in this photograph is the base of the original light that was finished in 1854. It was built of cast iron, which would seem an odd choice for such a corrosive environment.

In 1881, a similar tower on the Calf Rock to the north was broken off at the base by a storm, so the Fastnet was replaced before it could suffer a similar fate. The new tower is made of interlocking granite blocks and was completed in 1904.

Canon EOS 6D, EF24mm f/1.4L II USM

f/9, 1/800 at ISO 200

Streek Head, County Cork

Streek Head marks the entrance to Crookhaven, a well-sheltered anchorage right on the southwestern tip of Ireland. Historically, it was of great importance to the Atlantic shipping trade with ocean-going ships provisioning here.

It was also the place where Guglielmo Marconi built an antenna in his early attempts to get a wireless message across the Atlantic. He was not successful, but the village became an important telegraph station later.

After crossing from America, ships would stop here to find out where their cargo had been sold and therefore which port to head to.

Canon EOS 5D Mk III, EF24mm f/2.8 IS USM

f/4, 1/400 at ISO 100

Barley Cove, County Cork

Barley Cove is perhaps the best-loved beach in West Cork. A wonderful place for a family day out in pleasant weather, it can be ferocious in stormy weather.

This image was made on a pleasant day. Often the middle of the day is not the best time to photograph the landscape, but when the sort of clouds seen here are present, it opens up all sorts of possibilities.

In 1755, the Great Lisbon Earthquake generated a tsunami that caused widespread damage, even as far north as Ireland. It's believed that the tsunami left as part of its legacy the extensive sand dunes at Barley Cove.

Canon EOS 5D Mk III, EF24mm f/2.8 IS USM

f/8, 1/500 at ISO 100

Mizen Head, County Cork

At the extreme southwest corner of Ireland, Mizen Head is a wild, exposed place. It's home to a signal station and lighthouse, although the light is not housed in a tower but is merely a freestanding pillar at the western end of the buildings.

Mizen was originally established in 1909 as a fog signal station only. At that time, fog signals were made by detonating explosives at regular intervals.

However, in 1920 the IRA raided the station and stole the explosives. As a result, all fog signals around the coast were stopped for four years because their safety could not be guaranteed.

This image was made at sunrise on a calm morning.

Canon EOS 5D Mk III, EF24mm f/2.8 IS USM

f/4, 1/100 at ISO 100

Three Castle Head, County Cork

This headland is truly one of the hidden gems of the Atlantic coast. Three Castle Head is privately owned, but (as of this writing) walkers are permitted to roam from the road up to Dunlough Castle, which is just visible here in front of the lake on the head.

First founded around the 13th century, the ruins on the site are probably from the 15th century. The ruins include three keeps of dry stone construction and the remains of a curtain wall. The lake is also probably man made, as another wall at the eastern end appears to serve as a dam.

In this image, the land at the very left of the frame is the Sheep's Head peninsula, the smallest of the five major peninsulas that make up the coast of west Cork and Kerry.

Canon EOS 5D Mk III, EF24mm f/2.8 IS USM

f/8, 1/400 at ISO 100

Ardnakinna, County Cork

Located on the western tip of Bere Island, Ardnakinna guards the western entrance to Berehaven, the narrow channel between the island and the town of Castletownbere on the mainland.

Even though the lighthouse is on a relatively large, inhabited island close to the mainland, supplies and equipment must be airlifted in, as there is no road access, only a footpath.

However, the main depot for the Commissioners of Irish Lights in the southwest is located a stone's throw away in Castletownbere itself, so supplies don't have far to come.

Canon EOS 5D Mk III, EF24mm f/2.8 IS USM

f/4, 1/100 at ISO 100

Black Ball Head, County Cork

Black Ball Head is located towards the western end of the Beara peninsula and is remarkable only in the beauty of its surroundings and the impressive nature of the headland itself.

The tower on its summit is one of many that dot the Irish coast. This series of towers was built in the early 19th century as a semaphore signal network, primarily to give warning of any invasion by Napoleonic forces. If all were operational at the same time (which might not have been the case), in theory a signal from any one of them could travel all the way around the coast as far as Dublin.

Canon EOS 5D Mk III, EF24mm f/2.8 IS USM

f/4, 1/250 at ISO 100

Derrynane Beach, County Kerry

The Ring of Kerry, despite its reputation for amazing scenery actually bypasses many of the real gems of the Kerry landscape. However, Derrynane is an exception. It's most dramatically seen when coming from the north where the bay is revealed all at once, a playground of sheltered coves and islets, and of course, its famous beach.

Hard against the mountains of southwest Kerry, it's a place that rewards exploration. For this photograph, I wanted to capture a less obvious viewpoint, and found the meandering stream through the beach a compelling subject.

Can you spot the house built to look like a ship?

Canon EOS 5D Mk III, EF24mm f/2.8 IS USM

f/5.6, 1/320 at ISO 100

Puffin Island & Skelligs, County Kerry

This is a photograph I've long wanted. When photographing Puffin Island from the land, it's hard to properly separate it from the foreground, but from the air you can give it the space it needs. The lonely Skellig Islands are visible on the horizon, with Lemon Rock making an appearance off to the left.

Sunrise and sunset are very special times of the day and can be particularly appealing when the weather is unsettled. It's important to arrive early, though, because what can be a marvelous light show can often end too soon.

On this particular evening, the sun disappeared behind the bank of cloud sitting just on the horizon moments after I made this image, putting a premature end to the light show.

Canon EOS 5D Mk III, EF24mm f/2.8 IS USM

f/2.8, 1/320 at ISO 100

Valentia Island, County Kerry

Valentia Island is one of the more deceiving locations in Kerry. Seen from the land, it looks peaceful and pastoral with farms and houses dotted along a gently sloping hillside. It's only when you arrive on the island itself and explore it that its dual nature is revealed. From Geokaun and Cromwell Point in the east to Bray Head (pictured here) in the west, there is a wild coastline that faces north.

In this photograph, the tremendous cliffs show where the sea has eaten away at the hill over aeons. Just below the signal tower, although not visible in this photograph, are the remains of an EIRE marker. Several of these markers were placed along the coast during World War II to inform passing US airmen that they were crossing over Ireland.

Canon EOS 5D Mk III, EF24mm f/2.8 IS USM

f/2.8, 1/200 at ISO 100

Valentia Sound, County Kerry

This image, made on the same morning as the one on the facing page, shows more detail of the sound between Valentia and the mainland. The bridge that links the island to Portmagee can be clearly seen. The bridge was built in 1970, and previously a ferry ran from the village. At the eastern end of the island, a ferry still runs, connecting that side with the town of Cahersiveen.

In the distance, the snow-capped peaks of the Macgillycuddy's Reeks, Ireland's highest mountain range, huddle together beneath a squall.

Canon EOS 5D Mk III, EF24mm f/2.8 IS USM

f/2.8, 1/200 at ISO 100

Rossbeigh, County Kerry

Rossbeigh is a partner to Inch. It emerges from the Iveragh peninsula and, while thinner and shorter than its cousin, it's no less beautiful.

During the storms of 2013–2014, the facilities at the base of the spit were extensively damaged, and the shape of the peninsula was somewhat altered.

The beach is home to the wreck of the Sunbeam, a 19th century schooner that was driven ashore and wrecked here with no loss of life in 1904.

📷 Canon EOS 5D Mk III, EF24mm f/2.8 IS USM

f/5.6, 1/30 at ISO 200

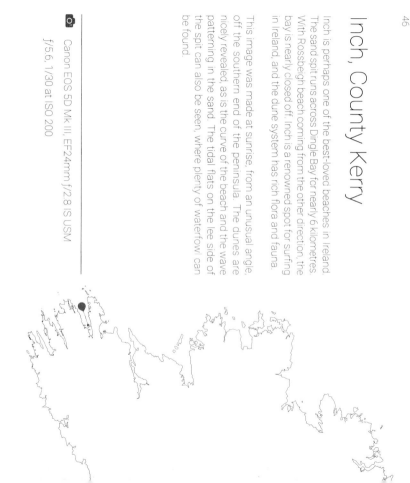

Inch, County Kerry

Inch is perhaps one of the best-loved beaches in Ireland. The sand spit runs across Dingle Bay for nearly 6 kilometres. With Rossbeigh beach coming from the other direction, the bay is nearly closed off. Inch is a renowned spot for surfing in Ireland, and the dune system has rich flora and fauna.

This image was made at sunrise, from an unusual angle, off of the southern end of the peninsula. The dunes are nicely revealed, as is the curve of the beach and the wave patterning in the sand. The tidal flats on the lee side of the spit can also be seen, where plenty of waterfowl can be found.

Canon EOS 5D Mk III, EF24mm f/2.8 IS USM

f/5.6, 1/30 at ISO 200

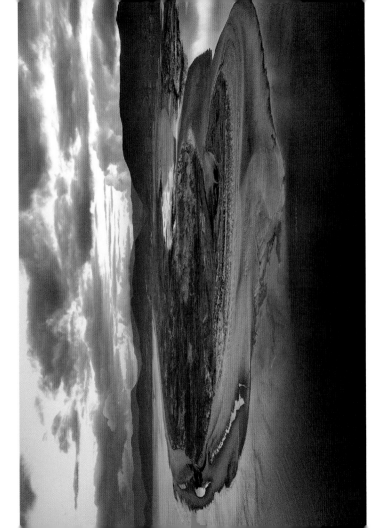

Dunmore Head, County Kerry

This part of the Kerry coast is one the keeps drawing me back. For my last book, The Irish Light, it took me five years to capture the cover image, which was photographed here. This aerial view shows the headland in context with the dramatic Blasket Islands. This is the westernmost part of the mainland of Ireland. Inis Tuaracht (pictured overleaf) is hidden behind the mass of the Great Blasket, with wisps of fog clinging to its summit.

The island to the right of the setting sun is Inis Tuaisceart, the Northern Island. It's also known locally as An Fear Marbh, the Dead Man. Or, less morbidly, the Sleeping Giant.

📷 Canon EOS 5D Mk III, EF24mm f/2.8 IS USM

f/5.6, 1/40 at ISO 200

Inis Tiaracht, County Kerry

I have a deep fascination with remote islands, and few are more interesting than Inis Tiaracht. The name means Western Island. This is the westernmost part of Ireland, and a place that few see properly, let alone visit.

The lighthouse was built in 1870, and two keepers, along with their families, lived on this inhospitable rock. It was initially a non-relieving station, meaning the keepers and their families lived here full time. In 1900, dwellings were built on Valentia Island and the keepers rotated on and off Inis Tiaracht. I can only imagine what it would have been like to be a child living here.

Also of interest is the westernmost railway in Europe, a funicular track that runs from the dwellings to the landing stage at the right side of the island under the lighthouse that was used to haul up supplies and equipment.

Canon EOS 6D, EF24mm f/1.4L II USM

f/5.6, 1/2000 at ISO 1600

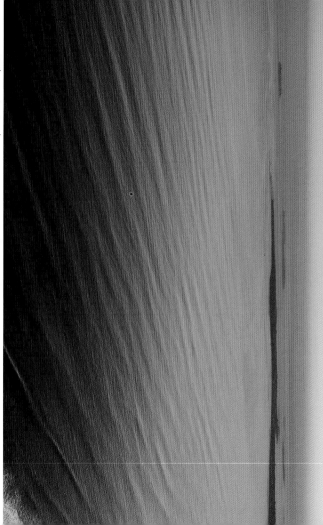

The Maharees at Sunrise, County Kerry

Another beloved location for holidaymakers and surfers is the Maharees, a 5 kilometre long peninsula off the north coast of the Dingle peninsula. It's actually a tombolo, a landform that occurs when an island or islands becomes attached to the shore by a spit of sand.

This photograph was made from the base of the peninsula, looking north just at sunrise. It

shows the wild dune system the dominates this part of the peninsula, with the early morning mist lying genty on the land.

Canon EOS 5D Mk III, EF24mm f/2.8 IS USM

f/5.6, 1/100 at ISO 200

The Maharees, County Kerry

This photograph was made from the end of the peninsula, looking south about an hour after sunrise on the same day the previous image was made.

As you can see, there's a significant difference, not just in the quality of light, but the landscape at this end of the peninsula is far more tamed and pastoral than the wild dunes of the southern end.

This image was made by stitching together two photographs made side by side, each capturing one side of the scene.

 Canon EOS 5D Mk III, EF24mm f/2.8 IS USM

f/5.6, 1/400 at ISO 200

Loop Head, County Clare

An often overlooked part of the west coast, Loop Head stands dramatically at the end of a long finger of land and guards the northern side of the Shannon Estuary. A lighthouse has stood here since the mid-1600s, and would originally have been a cottage type with a coal-burning brazier on the roof.

The lighthouse is still active, but like all those around the coast is now automated. The lightkeeper's house is in the care of the Irish Landmark Trust and can be rented for holiday stays.

The EIRE marker visible in this photograph was established in the 1940s as a guide to U.S. airmen transiting over the Atlantic. This one is in much better repair than most, as it is maintained by the local community.

Canon EOS 5D MK III, EF24mm f/2.8 IS USM

f/2.8, 1/40 at ISO 100

Kilkee, County Clare

The Cliffs of Moher get the lion's share of attention on Clare's coast. However, continuing south brings you to the Loop Head peninsula and Kilkee. The cliffs here might not be nearly as high as their more famous cousins, but what they lack in height they make up for in drama.

A drive from Kilkee to Loop Head is filled with bays, small high islands and sea stacks. In this image, looking north from Grean Rock, Bishop's Island is visible to the left. On this 60 metre high rock, largely inaccessible except to an intrepid climber, are the remains of an early Christian oratory, which dates from the 5th century.

Canon EOS 5D Mk III, EF24mm f/2.8 IS USM

f/4, 1/100 at ISO 100

Cliffs of Moher, County Clare

Easily the most recognisable of Irelands tourist attractions, the Cliffs of Moher are visited by huge numbers each year. Standing over 200 metres at their highest point, they are about a third the height of the highest sea cliffs in Ireland (that title goes to the cliffs at Croaghmore on Achill Island), but their sheer verticality is what makes them so spectacular.

Visible in this photograph is O'Brien's Tower, built in 1835, probably as an observation tower for Victorian tourists.

The massive sea stack of Branaunmore stands 67 metres high and must once have been connected to the cliffs by an arch. What a sight that would have been!

Canon EOS 5D Mk III, EF24mm f/2.8 IS USM

f/8, 1/160 at ISO 100

Dún Dúchathair, County Galway

Inis Mór, the largest of the three main Aran Islands, is replete with stone forts, including two dramatic coastal forts. Dún Dúchathair, or the Black Fort, lies on a spectacular promontory that juts out into the Atlantic.

It's not known if it was originally a promontory fort. Possibly, the bays on either side have dramatically enlarged in the thousands of years since the fort was built. It's also possible, although less likely, that the fort was not coastal at all, and was built some ways inland, and that the sea has advanced in the intervening time.

Regardless, it's a dramatic sight, and sees vastly less traffic than its busier and more famous cousin, Dún Aonghasa.

Canon EOS 5D Mk III, EF24mm f/2.8 IS USM

f/11, 1/30 at ISO 200

Dún Aonghasa, County Galway

Easily the most famous landmark on the Aran Islands, Dún Aonghasa on Inis Mór is magnificent. Perched nearly 100 metres above the foaming Atlantic, with massive thick stone walls, it's easy to see why so many people visit here each year. Indeed, most visitors to Inis Mór are daytrippers who want only to see this place and then leave the island–a real shame as there are many other amazing sights to see.

As a result of this popularity, during the middle of the day, the fort can be overrun with other tourists, somewhat spoiling the effect. I strongly recommend overnighting on the island and visiting at dawn, or at dusk, which is when this image was made. There is one person standing at the cliff edge in this image, which will give some idea of scale.

Canon EOS 5D Mk III, EF24mm f/2.8 IS USM

f/5.6, 1/40 at ISO 200

Dog's Bay, County Galway

Dog's Bay, like the Maharees in Dingle, is a tombolo, where two islands have naturally been joined to each other and the mainland by a sand spit. The result is a spectacular pair of bays, well sheltered from the sea and a safe place for water activities or just walking and admiring the view.

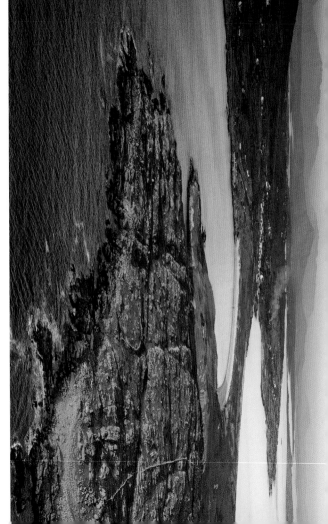

Dog's Bay is facing us in this image, and is the better of the beaches, nearly a mile long and with sand of crushed shells giving a beautiful white colour. The other side is known as Gurteen Bay.

📷 Canon EOS 5D Mk III, EF24mm f/2.8 IS USM

f/5.6, 1/100 at ISO 200

Slyne Head, County Galway

Slyne Head is a chain of islands off a peninsula on the Connemara coast. The name is an anglicisation of Ceann Léime, which means 'Leap Head'. This image was made just off the western end of the head, looking east. You can clearly see the two lighthouse towers, only one of which is still operational.

Originally, two towers were built, each with two lightkeeper's dwellings, to ensure that the lights were different enough from Clare Island so as not to cause confusion to mariners. They were completed in 1836, and the second tower was decommissioned in 1898.

Slyne is frequently lashed by storms, and despite its proximity to the mainland, reliefs could be delayed by several weeks in strong winter storms.

Canon EOS 5D Mk III, EF 24mm f/2.8 IS USM

f/5.6, 1/250 at ISO 200

Inisheeshan, County Galway

While searching for compositions, photographers look to the well-known locations. Sometimes the commonplace is just as beautiful. This island, just offshore at Slackport, is one such. I was scouting the area in advance of chartering a boat to go out to Slyne Head (visible at the top left of the image) the following morning. The weather was looking questionable, with a good swell running all through the day that would make our life difficult.

I headed out here, which is the nearest point of easy access to the head, to see what the waves were doing. The sunset was subtle but beautiful, and I hit upon this composition of the low, rocky islet pointing the way to Slyne Head while the sun sinks to the horizon.

Canon EOS 5D Mk III, EF24mm f/2.8 IS USM

f/5.6, 1/160 at ISO 200

Omey Island, County Galway

Omey Island, seen here with the Twelve Bens in the background, is only an island at high tide. The strand that separates it from the mainland can be easily crossed at low tide, and there are even stakes in the ground to mark out where you can drive across. You can see it in this image as a slightly lighter part of the water between the island and the mainland.

There is an annual horse race, the Omey Races, that is held on this strand. Start and end times vary due to the tide!

 Canon EOS 6D, EF24mm f/1.4L II USM

 f/6.3, 1/2500 at ISO 800

Ballynakill Harbour, County Galway

Ballynakill Harbour is adjacent to Letterfrack, a tourist hub for the nearby Connemara National Park. It sees few tourists, being off the beaten track. However, from the air it is a pleasing foreground for the Connemara hills in the background.

Diamond Hill is the prominent cone-shaped mountain in the centre of the image, with the Twelve Bens beyond. To its left, you can see straight down the Kylemore Glen with its abbey clinging to the slopes of Doughraugh Mountain to the left.

Canon EOS 5D Mk III, EF24mm f/2.8 IS USM

f/5.6, 1/800 at ISO 200

White Strand, County Mayo

There are two great strands on this part of the Mayo coast. Silver Strand and White Strand. Both are beautiful beaches, although access to White Strand can be difficult when the Owenadornaun River is running high.

The mountain in the background is Mweelrea, the highest mountain in Connaught. Because the mountain is so close to the coast, the weather can change dramatically and quickly. However, on this evening, the setting sun nicely illuminates the cap of cloud gracing its summit.

To the left of image, the entrance to the Doo Lough Valley can be seen with Barrclashcame forming its western wall, part of the Sheeffry Hills.

Canon EOS 5D Mk III, EF24mm f/2.8 IS USM

f/5.6, 1/80 at ISO 200

Roonagh Point, County Mayo

Marking the southern entrance to Clew Bay, Roonagh Point is the jumping-off point for Clare Island, which stands at the mouth of the bay. The pier is visible here at bottom left. It offers little protection from the Atlantic Swell, however, and sailings can often be canceled.

The dramatic cone of Croagh Patrick dominates the landscape, and the islands of Clew Bay can

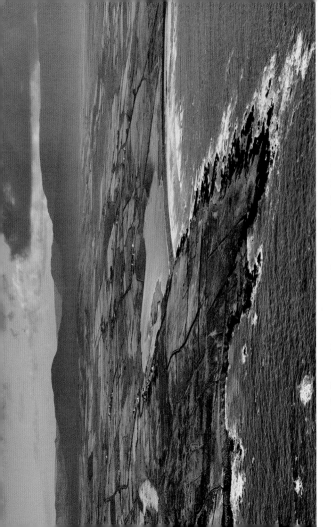

be seen to the left of image. You can even see the speck of white that is Inishgort Lighthouse, which marks the safe entrance to Westport Harbour in the maze of islands.

📷 Canon EOS 6D, EF24mm f/1.4L II USM

f/6.3, 1/2500 at ISO 800

Bertra Strand, County Mayo

Bertra is another sand spit, similar to Rossbeigh and Inch in Kerry. It juts out from the base of Croagh Patrick into the dramatic island-studded Clew Bay. Like many features along the coast, it suffered during the 2013-2014 winter storms, and the scars are visible where the grasses were stripped away by the relentless waves.

Out in the bay, the islands are known as drumlins, a feature left behind by the retreating glaciers at the end of the last ice age. Their rounded appearance gives the islands the look of whales surfacing to breathe.

Local tradition states that there are 365 islands in the bay, one for each day of the year. The actual number is disappointingly lower than that, at 117.

📷 Canon EOS 5D Mk III, EF24mm f/2.8 IS USM
f/5.6, 1/30 at ISO 200

Croagh Patrick, County Mayo

Possibly the most identifiable of Ireland's mountains, Croagh Patrick, locally known as the Reek, is beautiful, and never more so than when graced by a dusting of spring snow.

The Reek has been a place of pilgrimage for thousands of years. In 441 AD, St. Patrick is reputed to have fasted for forty days and nights on the summit. Each year thousands of people climb the mountain on Reek Sunday, the last Sunday in July, to commemorate his sacrifice.

The path left by all those feet, many of them bare on the sharp stony slopes, stands out very clearly on the slope

Canon EOS 5D Mk III, EF24mm f/2.8 IS USM

f/5.6, 1/1000 at ISO 200

Rainbow, Atlantic Ocean, County Mayo

This image was made on a helicopter flight to inspect offshore lighthouses along the west coast for damage following the winter storms of 2013-2014.

Rainbows in the air are not interrupted by the ground, and can form a complete circle if conditions are right. Alas, my lens wasn't sufficiently wide enough to capture the full circle.

but even a part of it is a spectacular sight. All rainbows are double rainbows, but only when the sun is strong enough does the second become visible.

Canon EOS 5D Mk II, EF14mm f/2.8L II USM

f/4, 1/2500 at ISO 800

Clare Island, County Mayo

Clare Island stands at the mouth of Clew Bay, its highest mountain, Knockmore, rising 462 metres from the water. The name is an anglicisation of the Irish Cnoc Mór which means Big Hill. So much for the romanticism of the Irish language!

The island is spectacular, even at the lower northern end where the lighthouse perches. It was built in 1806 but, like its cousin on Cape Clear Island in the south, it was sited too high and was frequently obscured by fog and low cloud. In 1965, a replacement light was placed on Achillbeg, just to the north across the sound. Clare Island's light was then extinguished for the last time, but the lighthouse remains and is now a bed and breakfast.

Canon EOS 5D Mk III, EF24mm f/2.8 IS USM

f/5.6, 1/800 at ISO 100

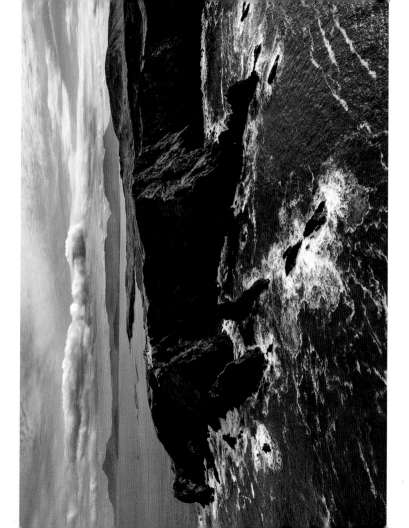

Achill Head, County Mayo

Achill is the largest of Ireland's offshore islands, and is close enough to the mainland that a bridge was built to it in 1887. That structure has been replaced twice since, with the newest being completed in 2008.

The island is a popular destination for outdoor and water sports enthusiasts. Keel Beach, which is just behind the right-hand ridge of Croaghaun, is a renowned surfing and kite surfing spot.

The island is also home to the highest sea cliffs in Ireland, which are visible in this image on the left side of the mountain peak of Croaghaun. Rising 688 metres, they are spectacular, but are not accessible by road and thus don't see many visitors.

Canon EOS 6D, EF24mm f/1.4L II USM

f/6.3, 1/2500 at ISO 800

Eagle Island, County Mayo

Where once two lighthouses stood, now only half of one remains on this storm-battered island. Two lights were built in 1835, but the eastern tower was abandoned in 1894 after it was damaged beyond repair in a storm, one of several to batter it over the years. One was so fierce that it filled the tower with water to the point that the keepers were unable to open the door. They needed to drill holes in the door to let the water escape before they could open it.

In recent years, the lantern room of the western tower was removed and the tower capped. A small LED beacon was put in its place, resulting in its shortened appearance in this image.

Canon EOS 5D Mk II, EF14mm f/2.8L II USM
f/5.6, 1/2000 at ISO 800

Benwee Head, County Mayo

Benwee offers some of the finest coastal scenery in Ireland but is not very well known. Seen in this image is Kid Island, with the dramatic Stags of Broadhaven in the background. This little archipelago of jagged rocks stands 97 metres tall at its highest, and is over 2 kilometres from shore

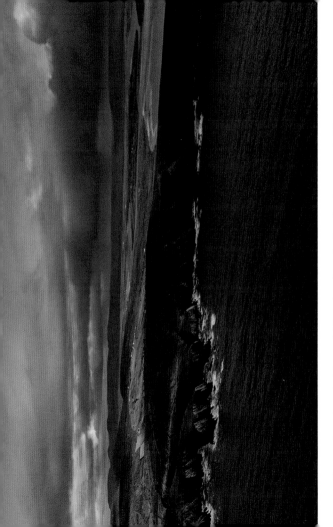

It rewards a closer look through binoculars from the headland, as several of the rocks have arches, and one is entirely bisected by a cave.

Canon EOS 5D Mk II, EF14mm f/2.8L II USM

f/7.1, 1/1600 at ISO 800

Dún Briste, County Mayo

This is the sea stack known as Dún Briste, which means Broken Fort. It stands 50 meters above sea level, and was once connected to the mainland by an arch that collapsed in 1393 due to heavy seas. A more colourful story states that St Patrick himself caused the collapse.

In the story, Crom Dubh, a god in legend, but in this tale a mere man, once lived here and refused to convert to Christianity. St. Patrick struck the arch with his staff, separating Dún Briste from the mainland. Crom Dubh and his son had to remain there "until the midges and the scaldcrows had eaten the flesh off their bones".[1]

In 1980, a team landed by helicopter on the stack and found the remains of two stone buildings. Crom's house?

Douglas Hyde, *Legends of Saints & Sinners: Collected and Translated from the Irish*

📷 Canon EOS 5D Mk III, EF24mm f/2.8 IS USM

f/5.6, 1/80 at ISO 200

Mullaghmore, County Sligo

This is an atypical image of Mullaghmore, a rocky headland on the Sligo coast. Pictured is Bunduff Strand, on the eastern side of the headland. This was an unplanned image. While flying over Sligo from Fanad Head to Sligo airport, I spotted the twisting shape of the river on the beach and scrambled to get the camera ready. I love how the landscape can hold surprises like this.

Mullaghmore is a hugely popular spot for surfers and is one of the best big wave destinations in the world, with waves as high as 15 metres.

 Canon EOS 6D, EF24mm f/1.4L II USM

f/5.6, 1/800 at ISO 400

Benbulben, County Sligo

Probably Ireland's most distinctive mountain, Benbulben towers over the coast of Sligo. It's a place that I'd long wanted to photograph, but the proper conditions had always eluded me. On this evening, the setting sun threw a wonderful golden light over its slopes.

The low light and long shadows that it creates reveal the tiny white dots of sheep grazing on the mountain.

In the background is Benwiskin, another beautiful and distinctive mountain in this range.

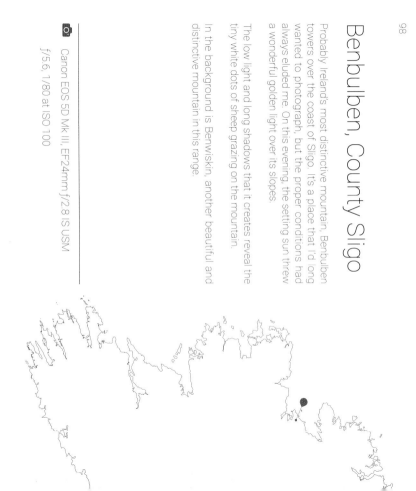

Canon EOS 5D Mk III, EF24mm f/2.8 IS USM

f/5.6, 1/80 at ISO 100

St. John's Point, County Donegal

There are two St. John's Points with lighthouses in Ireland: the one in this image, and one in County Down in Northern Ireland. This one is situated at the end of an 11 kilometre-long peninsula, probably one of the longest in Ireland. The light was first exhibited in 1831 and was converted to automatic operation in 1932, probably one of the very first in Ireland.

This image was made on a midsummer morning, and the sun has risen almost exactly in line with the peninsula as it extends to the northeast. Look closely and you will see scaffolding around the tower, which was at the time being renovated as part of a tourism initiative to make it self-catering accommodation.

Canon EOS 5D Mk III, EF24mm f/2.8 IS USM

f/4, 1/500 at ISO 100

Slieve League, County Donegal

Slieve League boasts some of the highest sea cliffs in Ireland, towering over 600 metres above the Atlantic Ocean. It's a popular spot for hillwalkers, boasting the famous One Man's Pass, a short section of ridge with dizzying drops on either side and just wide enough for just one person to walk along it.

The tower in these photographs is part of the network of signal stations built around the coast during the Napoleonic wars to warn of an invading fleet.

There are early Christian monastic remains on the mountain, and it's believed that monks sailed from the nearby village of Teelin to Iceland, landing there before the Viking settlement in the 9th century.

Canon EOS 5D Mk III, EF24mm f/2.8 IS USM

f/5.6, 1/30 at ISO 100

Arranmore, County Donegal

Arranmore is one of the most subtly dramatic lighthouses in Ireland. Seen from the island itself or from the south, it doesn't look like much. But from the north, as in this image, with the jagged fins of rock running towards you, fewer sights are more arresting.

The island is the second largest around the coast, after Achill in Mayo. Sadly, like most offshore islands in Ireland, it's experiencing a population decline as young people move away, and there's a lack of new people moving there to balance out the emigration.

Canon EOS 5D Mk II, EF14mm f/2.8L II USM

f/4, 1/800 at ISO 800

Tory Island, County Donegal

Tory is the northernmost of the inhabited islands

Here, we're looking at the eastern side of the island, known as Dún Bhalóir (Balor's Fort). The tower on the left of the image is An Tor Mór, or the Big Tower, and at about 80 metres it is the highest point on the island.

The prominent peak in the background, just below and to the left of the flight of birds, is Mount Errigal.

Canon EOS 5D Mk III, EF24mm f/2.8 IS USM

f/5.6, 1/100 at ISO 160

Magheroarty, County Donegal

This image looks out from above the Dooey Peninsula. Tory Island is the long, thin island at the top of the image. The pier at Magheroarty from which boats depart to the island is at the extreme middle left.

The scattering of islands in between the peninsula and Tory are dominated by Inishbofin,

which consists of two lobes connected by a narrow isthmus. It shares its name with another island in Galway.

 Canon EOS 6D, EF24mm f/1.4L II USM

f/5, 1/640 at ISO 1600

Boyeeghter Strand, County Donegal

No road gives access to Boyeeghter Strand. Known locally as The Murder Hole, the story involves a local woman, an English soldier, and a fatal fall from the cliffs.

Boyeeghter Strand is on the west side of Melmore at the northern tip of the Rosguill Peninsula, but there are no signposts to direct visitors there. However, it rewards the determined adventurer who's willing to make the roughly 20 minute walk across the dunes to reach it.

Canon EOS 5D Mk III, EF24mm ƒ/2.8 IS USM
ƒ/13, 1/100 at ISO 100

Fanad Head, County Donegal

Fanad is one of the most iconic lighthouses around the coast. The beautiful white tower and well-maintained dwellings set against the grassy headland play a big part of that. It also presents a beautiful aspect from the landward side. It's a wonderful subject for aerial photography, as from the land there are a limited number of viewpoints. The aerial dimension adds huge freedom of choice to the photographer.

On this evening, I placed the setting sun behind the lantern; a different sort of light than what usually shines through it!

If you look closely, you can see some local fishermen at work on the landing to the left of the tower.

Canon EOS 5D Mk III, EF24mm f/2.8 IS USM

f/3.5, 1/100 at ISO 100

Great Pollet Arch, County Donegal

Another location that particularly rewards the aerial perspective is the Great Pollet Arch. Long a favourite of landscape photographers, it's only a short hop down the coast from Fanad Head. There are no signs directing the wanderer to this spot, however, and the arch itself is on private land.

The arch is most often photographed from the beach seen here just behind the stack, and the views are generally looking out to sea. Taking to the air and looking the other direction shows the arch in context.

On this morning, I was very lucky with the sunrise. The sun came up in a clear patch of sky, illuminating both cloud and land with a wonderful, golden glow.

Canon EOS 5D Mk III, EF24mm f/2.8 IS USM

f/3.2, 1/100 at ISO 125

Banba's Crown, County Donegal

Banba's Crown is the very northernmost point of the Irish mainland. Malin Head is a little further west and a kilometre or so south. Once again we see one of the now-familiar Napoleonic watchtowers sitting on the hill.

This image was made right around the autumnal equinox. At this time of the year, the sun rises directly in the east and sets directly west, and so we're looking straight west in this photograph. The northernmost point of Ireland, therefore, is the rightmost rocks in the photograph.

When there's strong solar activity, the Northern Lights can be seen from Donegal, and Banba's Crown becomes very crowded with people hoping to catch a glimpse of this rare phenomenon.

Canon EOS 5D Mk III, EF24mm f/2.8 IS USM

f/3.5, 1/100 at ISO 100

Inishtrahull, County Donegal

Inishtrahull is the northernmost inhabitable island in Ireland, exceeded only by the Tor rocks about 1 kilometre to the north. The lonely outpost of Rockall is much further north still, but is contested between Ireland and Scotland.

This island was inhabited until 1929, when it was evacuated. The story is that illegal fishing by French, Scottish and English boats made it impossible for the remaining people, who relied on fishing for their living, to live there, and so only the lightkeepers remained.

There has been a light here since 1812, and it was built on the eastern side of the island. In 1905, a fog signal was established on the western end. In 1957 the old tower on the east end was demolished and replaced with the new lighthouse adjacent to the fog station, pictured here.

Canon EOS 6D, EF24mm f/1.4L II USM

f/5.6, 1/4000 at ISO 400

Afterword

This is my second book, after The Irish Light, and the first that was its own project. The Irish Light was a collection of existing photographs and required only that I select those I wanted to include and lay them out in a pleasing manner. Despite this, the project took a lot of work to get just right.

For this book, I knew the challenge would be greater, as I had only a handful of images to put towards it when I decided to go ahead, sometime in March 2014. I set an aggressive deadline of March 2015 to go to print, but it rapidly became clear that was unrealistic. I lead several photography workshops throughout the year, and between problems with the drone and my travel, I was unable to really start work until September 2014.

At that time, I thought that aerial photography would form a significant part of the book, but it wouldn't be the sole subject. On my first trip, which was to Donegal, I was very successful and got six or seven images with the drone that I was happy with. I made the decision at that point, while still in the field, that the new book would be entirely comprised of aerial photographs. I had a number of images that would serve as the backbone of the book from a flight I did with the Commissioners of Irish Lights in January 2014. That winter saw a series of destructive storms pass over Ireland, damaging infrastructure up and down the coast.

I got a phone call one afternoon saying that there was a flight being made along the entire coast to check for damage on the offshore lighthouses, and would I be interested in coming along? The caller was apologetic for the short notice, but I couldn't say "yes" fast enough. Such opportunities come along very rarely, and while I'd been out on hops to all the southwestern stations in the past, I'd never been to any of the others off the west coast.

That flight was quite the experience, taking three days to travel from the Bull Rock off the coast of Cork to Inishtrahull off Donegal. This allowed me to photograph many of the normally inaccessible lighthouses. Unfortunately, the light wasn't great for much of the trip and therefore not all the lighthouses have made it into this book. Perhaps that's a project for another year. I realized as I made the decision to fill this book with only aerial photographs that I was taking a gamble. I knew that I was fortunate with the weather on that first trip and was very aware that I would need to make most of the photographs during winter—not a time that's known to be particularly forgiving on the Atlantic coast.

Not only can drones not fly in rain, but they are limited by wind to a greater degree than full-size aircraft. And wind and rain I would have in abundance! However, on subsequent trips I was fortunate. The weather in winter tends to be squally and changeable. It may be pouring rain and blowing a gale on one day, but the next may be far more moderate.

As the trips went by, I was able to fill the blank space in the book piece by piece. Finally, in early May I made several forays up and down the coast, filling the time I should have been at home with my family between photography workshops with travels for the book.

And then, it was done. I had all the images I needed, and it was time to finalize the layout. There's something very pleasing about seeing all the pieces come together and the blank pages in the document vanish, one after the other. A great sense of relief descends when the last page is filled and the book is complete.

I've had a wonderful time on this project. It has been exhilarating, terrifying, tedious at times, sometimes even contemplative. But ultimately very rewarding. As I write this, it's seven days before my printing deadline, and I'm filling in these words during a quiet moment after a full night shooting in Iceland. I think, for my next book, that I'll allow a little more time to complete the project!

I hope you enjoyed the book as much as I've enjoyed making it.

Peter Cox

Hellnar, Snæfellsnes, Iceland

June 2015

Acknowledgements

No project like this is done in a vacuum, especially not one that is done on such a tight timescale and with such new technology.

First and foremost, I have to thank my wife, Ann. Without her support, this would not have been possible. She works full time and, when I'm not around, is solely responsible for our nearly five-year-old son, Liam. Despite my ridiculous travel schedule between photography workshops and trips for this book, she has remained continually patient, gracious, and uncomplaining under the pressure this puts her under. I'm constantly in her debt.

To Liam, I must also give thanks and an apology for being away so much, even if it does mean more TV time than when I'm around! His enthusiastic greetings when I come home don't make up for the time lost with him, but it definitely puts a salve on the wound.

To my mother, dead since 2009, and my father, dead since 2007, I owe a special thanks. After moving home in 2005 from the US, I was unsure what direction to take. I no longer enjoyed the IT work I had made a career of, and was wistfully imagining what it might be like to become a professional photographer. It was my mother's strong assertion that I should pursue that goal that made it seem attainable, and I'm not sure if I would have gone down this road if not for that conversation. My father was always supportive of whatever decisions I made, and while making this book I trod some old ground where previously I had spent holidays with him in my youth. Many a glass of milk and packet of fig rolls were consumed in his honour.

To the rest of my family I'm also very grateful. I'm lucky enough to have two sisters and a brother who are all great friends, and we support each other strongly. For their help in all things, I thank them.

For direct help in making this book possible, I have to thank the Commissioners of Irish Lights for their generous assistance in getting me out to the remote lighthouses that I have such a strong attraction towards. There's so much tradition and history in these places, and I'm so glad to have been able to taste a little of it before it disappears entirely.

For his service above and beyond the call of duty, I have to thank Damien Doyle of Copter Snop Ireland. He kept me flying despite several failures both bizarre and mundane, and even went so far as to lend me his personal drone when my own was lost, so that I could finish the book in time. I'm sure he groaned inwardly whenever my number came up on his phone, but he was never anything but cheery and helpful. Most of the time, anyway!

A hearty thanks is also due to Elizabeth Wilde, who picked up the task of editing the book at a very late stage and turned it around on a dime. She did a fantastic job of guiding me to the finish line and ensuring the quality of the final result. She also made some very valuable suggestions on the structure and layout of the photographs.

Lastly, I must thank the Kickstarter backers who funded this book. I turned to crowd funding for my first book, The Irish Light, and was amazed at the response. When I launched the campaign for this book, I was not expecting anywhere near the same level of support. I was humbled and very gratified to see it reach even more people: over 700 backers!

My thanks to you all, and I hope that you enjoy what your support has made

Notable Kickstarter Contributors:

Alan Cox, Ronadh Cox, Margaret Wu, John Scanlan, Carol and Sean Landers,

Kevin Raber, M. W. Schroeder, Doug Dinkle, Nicholas Schoeder, Noel Power,

George Allan, Michele and David Gough, Ciaran O'Donnell, Gary Griffin,

John Law, Brian Gaynor, Vicki Hsu, Rick and Jean Mofsen, Scott A. Schollenberger,

Jay and Deb Yocis, Dave Schaffelburg, Stephen M. Byrne, Damien Kelleher,

Bob Haugh from Travel Department, Rhonda Troutman, Mel Foody, Howard Stevens,

Fionnuala Gibney, Miles Flint, Klaus Blumhofer, Conor Crotty, Scott Hillmann,

Mick Murphy, Mike Johnson, Andrew E. Nixon

Major Kickstarter Contributors:

David and Joanie O'Reilly, Richard Walsh